D0366879

ROYAL COURT

Royal Court Theatre presents

DUBLIN CAROL

by **Conor McPherson**

First performed by the Royal Court at The Old Vic,
Waterloo Road, London on 15 January 2000

First performance at the Royal Court Jerwood Theatre Downstairs,
Sloane Square, London on 17 February 2000

DUBLIN CAROL

by **Conor McPherson**

Cast in order of appearance
Mark **Andrew Scott**
John **Brian Cox**
Mary **Bronagh Gallagher**

Director **Ian Rickson**
Designer **Rae Smith**
Lighting Designer **Paule Constable**
Music **Stephen Warbeck**
Sound Designer **Paul Arditti**
Assistant Director **Yvonne McDevitt**
Casting Director **Lisa Makin**
Production Manager **Paul Handley**
Company Stage Manager **Cath Binks**
Stage Management **Jayne Aplin, Jon Howard**
Assistant Stage Manager **Charlotte E Padgham**
Company Voice Work **Patsy Rodenburg**
Dialect Coach **Joan Washington**
Costume Supervisor **Iona Kenrick**
Set Construction **Scott Fleary Ltd**
Set Painter **Paddy Hamilton**
Production Photography **Ivan Kyncl**

Royal Court Theatre wishes to thank the following for their help with this production: For background research: Professor Anthony Clare, Dr Miriam Stoppard, John Stafford at Stafford and Son Ltd, Conor Massey. Wardrobe care by Persil and Comfort courtesy of Lever Brothers Ltd.

THE COMPANY

Conor McPherson (writer)
For the Royal Court: The Weir.
Theatre includes: This Lime Tree Bower, St
Nicholas (Bush); The Good Thief, Rum and
Vodka (Fly by Night Theatre Company, Dublin).
Radio: This Lime Tree Bower, The Weir.
Film: I Went Down, Saltwater.

Paul Arditti (sound designer)
Paul Arditti has been designing sound for theatre
since 1983. He currently combines his post as
Head of Sound at the Royal Court (where he has
designed more than 40 productions) with regular
freelance projects.
For the Royal Court: The Kitchen, Rat in the
Skull, Some Voices, Mojo, The Lights, The Weir,
The Steward of Christendom, Shopping and
Fucking, Blue Heart, (co-productions with Out
of Joint). The Chairs (co-production with
Theatre de Complicite); The Strip, Never Land,
Cleansed, Via Dolorosa, Real Classy Affair and
the 1998 Young Writers' Festival 'Choice'.
Other theatre includes: Our Lady of Sligo (RNT
with Out of Joint); Some Explicit Polaroids (Out
of Joint); Hamlet, The Tempest (RSC); Orpheus
Descending, Cyrano de Bergerac, St Joan (West
End); Marathon (Gate).
Musicals include: Doctor Dolittle, Piaf, The
Threepenny Opera.
Awards include: Drama Desk Award for
Outstanding Sound Design 1992 for Four
Baboons Adoring the Sun (Broadway).

Paule Constable (lighting designer)
For the Royal Court: The Weir, The Glory of
Living.
Other theatre includes: Tales from Ovid, The
Dispute, Uncle Vanya, Beckett 'Shorts' , The
Mysteries (RSC); The Darker Face of the Earth,
Haroun and the Sea of Stories, Caucasian Chalk
Circle (RNT); Amadeus (West End, Broadway,
Olivier nomination); Les Misérables (Tel Aviv);
Playhouse Creatures (Old Vic); More Grimms'
Tales (Young Vic and New York); four
productions for Theatre de Complicité including
the Olivier-nominated Street of Crocodiles.
Opera includes: ENO, Welsh National Opera,
Scottish Opera, Opera North, New Zealand
International Festival.

Brian Cox
For the Royal Court: Cromwell, Hedda Gabler,
In Celebration, Rat in the Skull (and Broadway).
Other Theatre includes: Art (Royale Theatre,
New York); Skylight (Mark Taper Forum, LA); St
Nicholas (The Bush, London / Primary Stages,
New York); The Music Man (Regent's Park /
Tour); The Master Builder (Lyceum, Edinburgh /
Riverside); King Lear, Richard III (RNT); Frankie
and Johnny (Comedy Theatre); The Taming of
the Shrew, Titus Andronicus, Fashion, Penny for
a Song, Misalliance, Danton (RSC); The
Deliberate Death of a Polish Priest (Almeida
Theatre); Strange Interlude (Duke of York's and
Broadway); Moby Dick, Danton's Death, Have
You Anything to Declare? (Royal Exchange
Manchester); Summer Party (Crucible,
Sheffield); Macbeth (Cambridge Theatre
Company); Herod, Julius Caesar (RNT); Brand
(Nottingham Playhouse); Getting On (Queens).
Television inlcudes: The Cup, Nuremburg,
Longitude, Family Brood, Food for Ravens, Red
Dwarf, Witness against Hitler, Picasso, The
Negotiator, Sean's Show, Pigboy, Sharpe's Rifles,
Inspector Morse, Grushko, Six Characters in
Search of an Author, The Big Battalions, Redfox,
Van der Valk, The Lost Language of the Cranes,
Secret Weapon, Shadow of the Sun, The
Cloning of Joanna May, Perfect Scoundrels, Alias
Smith and Jones, Rat in the Skull, Shoot for the
Sun, Home Cooking, The Fourth Floor, Bach,
Jemima Shore, Crown Court, Minder, The
House on the Hill, Therese Raquin, Bothwell,
Dalhouse's Luck, Churchill's People, The Devils,
Crown: Henry II, Changeling, Master of
Ballantrae.
Films include: Strictly Sinatra, Complicity, The
Minus Man, Mad about Mambo, The Corrupter,
The Boxer, Desperate Measures, Rushmore,
Kiss the Girls, The Glimmer Man, Chain
Reaction, The Long Kiss Goodnight, Rob Roy,
Braveheart, Prince of Jutland, Iron Will, Hidden
Agenda, Manhunter, Pope John, Florence
Nightingale.

Bronagh Gallagher
For the Royal Court: Portia Coghlan (with
Abbey, Dublin).
Other theatre includes: The Fitz (Lyric
Hammersmith); Street of Crocodiles (Theatre
de Complicite); Caucasian Chalk Circle
(RNT/Compicite Tour); The Iceman Cometh, A
Crucial Week in the Life of a Grocer's Assistant,
A Patriot Game (Abbey, Dublin); Peer Gynt
(Thelma Holt Productions); The Rocky Horror
Show (SFX Centre, Dublin).
Television includes: Deja Vu, Cry Wolf, The
Shadow of a Gunman, Ruffian Hearts, Over the
Rainbow, The Bill, You, Me and Marley, Flash
Mcveigh, Island of Strangers, Dear Sarah.
Film includes: Thanks for the Memories, This
Year's Love, Star Wars, Divorcing Jack, Painted
Angels, Pulp Fiction, Mary Reilly, The
Commitments, The Most Fertile Man in Ireland.

Yvonne McDevitt (assistant director)
As Assistant: The Weir (Royal Court); The
Meeting, Kill the Old Torture the Young, Perfect
Days (Traverse); The Invisible Woman (Gate);
Madame Butterfly (Robert Wilson, L'Opera
Bastille).
As Director: Acts (Traverse); The Lottery Ticket
(The Red Room); Not I, Rockaby (Dublin Fringe
Festival / Hermitage, Moscow).

Ian Rickson (director)
Ian Rickson is the Artistic Director of the Royal
Court.
For the Royal Court: The Weir (Theatre
Upstairs and Theatre Downstairs), The Lights,
Pale Horse, Mojo (& Steppenwolf Theatre Co.,
Chicago), Ashes and Sand, Some Voices, Killers
(1992 Young Writers' Festival), Wildfire.
Other theatre includes: The Day I Stood Still
(RNT); The House of Yes (Gate Theatre,
London); Me and My Friend (Chichester Festival
Theatre); Queer Fish (BAC); First Strike (Soho
Poly).
Opera includes: La Serva Padrona (Broomhill).

Andrew Scott
Theatre includes: The Lonesome West (Druid);
Long Day's Journey Into Night, (Gate, Dublin:
Irish Times Award Nomination for Best
Supporting Actor / Spirit of Life Award Actor of
the Year '98); The Secret Fall of Constance
Wilde (Abbey / Melbourne Arts Festival); The
Marriage of Figaro, A Woman of No Importance,
Six Characters in Search of an Author (Abbey,
Dublin); All My Sons, Brighton Beach Memoirs
(Andrew's Lane, Dublin); The Best of Broadway
(Rupert Guinness Theatre, Dublin).
Television includes: Longitude, The American.
Film includes: Nora, Saving Private Ryan, The
Cigarette Girl, Sweety Barrett, Miracle at
Midnight, Drinking Crude, The Budgie, Korea.
Radio includes: Romeo and Juliet, The Two
Gallants, A Shout in the Distance, I Want To Go
Home.

Rae Smith (designer)
For the Royal Court: The Weir, Some Voices,
Trust.
Other theatre includes: Cause Celebre,
Sarasine, Mrs Warren's Profession, A Christmas
Carol, The Letter (Lyric Hammersmith); The
Cocktail Party, A Midsummer Night's Dream
(Lyceum, Edinburgh); Endgame, Juno and the
Paycock (Donmar Warehouse); Silence, Silence,
Silence (Mladinsko Theatre, Slovenia); The
Phoenician Women, Henry IV (RSC); The Visit,
Help I'm Alive, Ave Maria, The Street of
Crocodiles (Theatre de Complicite).
Opera includes: Don Giovanni (Welsh National
Opera); The Magic Flute (Opera North);
Shameless (Opera Circus); The Maids (Lyric
Hammersmith).
Rae has also directed and designed Lucky
(David Glass Ensemble); Mysteria (RSC) and is
currently working on The Terminatrix (National
Theatre Studio / ENO). She has received two
design awards for working sabbaticals in
Indonesia and Japan. Future productions include:
La Finta Semplice (Royal Opera House Studio);
The Way of The World (Royal Exchange,
Manchester).
www.rae-smith.co.uk

Stephen Warbeck (composer)
For the Royal Court : Glory of Living, The
Lights, Harry and Me, Pale Horses, Rat in the
Skull, Mojo, Simpatico, The Editing Process, The
Kitchen, Blood, Greenland, Bloody Poetry, A
Lie of the Mind, Built on Sand.
Theatre music includes: The Prime of Miss Jean
Brodie, The Day I Stood Still, Light Shining in
Buckinghamshire, An Inspector Calls, Machinal,
The Mother, Roots, Magic Olympical Games, At
Our Table (RNT); The Tempest, Romeo and
Juliet, The White Devil, The Taming of the
Shrew, The Cherry Orchard, Cymbeline (RSC);
Figaro Gets Divorced, Pioneers & Purgatory in
Ingolstadt, Damned For Despair, Canterbury
Tales, Judgement Day (Gate).
Television includes: A Christmas Carol, Bright
Hair, The Student Prince, Element of Doubt,
Truth or Dare, Nervous Energy, Prime Suspect,
In the Border Country, Roots, Nona, You, Me
and Marley, Happy Feet, Bitter Harvest, The
Changeling, Skallagrigg.
Film includes: Mystery Men, Fanny and Elvis,
Shakespeare In Love, Heart, My Son the Fanatic,
Mrs Brown, Different For Girls, Brothers in
Trouble, O Mary This London, Sister My Sister.
Current film projects include: Dancer, Quills,
Pavarotti in Dad's Room.
Awards include: Academy Award and BAFTA
Nomination for Best Original Musical or
Comedy Score for Shakespeare in Love.
Stephen has also written music for many BBC
Radio plays, writes for his band the hKippers
and the Metropolitan Water Board.

THE ENGLISH STAGE COMPANY AT THE ROYAL COURT

The English Stage Company at the Royal Court opened in 1956 as a subsidised theatre producing new British plays, international plays and some classical revivals.

The first artistic director George Devine aimed to create a writers' theatre, 'a place where the dramatist is acknowledged as the fundamental creative force in the theatre and where the play is more important than the actors, the director, the designer'. The urgent need was to find a contemporary style in which the play, the acting, direction and design are all combined. He believed that 'the battle will be a long one to continue to create the right conditions for writers to work in'.

Devine aimed to discover 'hard-hitting, uncompromising writers whose plays are stimulating, provocative and exciting'. The Royal Court production of John Osborne's Look Back in Anger in May 1956 is now seen as the decisive starting point of modern British drama, and the policy created a new generation of British playwrights. The first wave included John Osborne, Arnold Wesker, John Arden, Ann Jellicoe, N F Simpson and Edward Bond. Early seasons included new international plays by Bertolt Brecht, Eugène Ionesco, Samuel Beckett, Jean-Paul Sartre and Marguerite Duras.

The theatre started with the 400-seat proscenium arch Theatre Downstairs, and then in 1969 opened a second theatre, the 60-seat studio Theatre Upstairs. Productions in the Theatre Upstairs have transferred to the West End, such as Conor McPherson's The Weir, Kevin Elyot's My Night With Reg and Ariel Dorfman's Death and the Maiden. The Royal Court also co-produces plays which have transferred to the West End or toured internationally, such as Sebastian Barry's The Steward of Christendom and Mark Ravenhill's Shopping and Fucking (with Out of Joint), Martin McDonagh's The Beauty Queen Of Leenane (with Druid Theatre Company), Ayub Khan-Din's East is East (with Tamasha Theatre Company, and now a feature film).

Since 1994 the Royal Court's artistic policy has again been vigorously directed to finding a new generation of playwrights. The writers include Joe Penhall, Rebecca Prichard, Michael Wynne, Nick Grosso, Judy Upton, Meredith Oakes, Sarah Kane, Anthony Neilson, Judith Johnson, James Stock, Jez Butterworth, Simon Block, Martin McDonagh, Mark Ravenhill, Ayub Khan-Din, Tamantha Hammerschlag, Jess Walters, Conor McPherson, Simon Stephens, Richard Bean, Roy Williams, Gary Mitchell, Mick Mahoney, Simon Stephens, Rebecca Gilman, Christopher Shinn and Kia Corthron. This expanded programme of new plays has been made possible through the support of the Jerwood Foundation, and many in association with the Royal National Theatre Studio.

In recent years there have been record-breaking productions at the box office, with capacity houses for Jez Butterworth's Mojo, Sebastian Barry's The Steward of Christendom, Martin McDonagh's The Beauty Queen of Leenane, Ayub Khan-Din's East is East, Eugène Ionesco's The Chairs. Conor McPherson's The Weir transferred to the West End in October 1998, is now running at the Duke of York's Theatre.

The newly refurbished theatre in Sloane Square opened in January 2000, with a policy still inspired by the first artistic director George Devine. The Royal Court is an international theatre for new plays and new playwrights, and the work shapes contemporary drama in Britain and overseas.

RECENT AWARDS

At the 1998 Tony Awards, Martin McDonagh's The Beauty Queen of Leenane (co-production with Druid Theatre Company) won four awards including Garry Hynes for Best Director and was nominated for a further two. Eugène Ionesco's The Chairs (co-production with Theatre de Complicite) was nominated for six Tony awards. David Hare won the 1998 Time Out Live Award for Outstanding Achievement for Via Dolorosa. Sarah Kane won the 1998 Arts Foundation Fellowship in Playwriting. Rebecca Prichard won the 1998 Critics' Circle Award for Most Promising Playwright for Yard Gal.

Conor McPherson won the 1999 Olivier Award for Best New Play for The Weir. The Royal Court won the 1999 ITI Award for Excellence in International Theatre. Sarah Kane's Cleansed was nominated Best Foreign Language Play in 1999 by Theater Heute in Germany. Rebecca Gilman won the 1999 Evening Standard Award for Most Promising Playwright for The Glory of Living.

In 1999, the Royal Court won the European theatre prize New Theatrical Realities, presented at Taormina Arte in Sicily, for its efforts in recent years in discovering and producing the work of young British dramatists.

RE-BUILDING THE ROYAL COURT

In 1995, the Royal Court was awarded a National Lottery grant through the Arts Council of England, to pay for three quarters of a £26 m project to re-build completely our 100-year old home. The rules of the award required the Royal Court to raise £7.5 m in partnership funding. The building has been completed thanks to the generous support of those listed below. We are particularly grateful for the contributions of over 5,000 audience members.

If you would like to support the ongoing work of the Royal Court please contact the Development Department on 020 7565 5050.

ROYAL COURT
DEVELOPMENT BOARD
Elisabeth Murdoch (Chair)
Jonathan Cameron (Vice Chair)
Timothy Burrill
Anthony Burton
Jonathan Caplan QC
Victoria Elenowitz
Monica Gerard-Sharp
Joyce Hytner
Feona McEwan
Michael Potter
Sue Stapely
Charlotte Watcyn Lewis

PRINCIPAL DONOR
Jerwood Foundation

WRITERS CIRCLE
BSkyB Ltd
The Cadogan Estate
Carillon/Schal
News International plc
Pathé
The Eva and Hans K Rausing Trust
The Rayne Foundation
Garfield Weston Foundation

DIRECTORS CIRCLE
The Esmée Fairbairn Charitable Trust
The Granada Group plc

ACTORS CIRCLE
Ronald Cohen & Sharon Harel-Cohen
Quercus Charitable Trust
The Basil Samuel Charitable Trust
The Trusthouse Charitable Foundation
The Woodward Charitable Trust

SPECIFIC DONATIONS
The Foundation for Sport and the Arts for Stage System
John Lewis Partnership plc for Balcony
City Parochial Foundation for Infra Red Induction Loops and Toilets for Disabled Patrons
RSA Art for Architecture Award Scheme for Antoni Malinowski Wall Painting
Theatre Restoration Fund

STAGE HANDS CIRCLE
Anonymous
Miss P Abel Smith
The Arthur Andersen Foundation
Associated Newspapers Ltd
The Honorable M L Astor Charitable Trust
Rosalind Bax
Character Masonry Services Ltd
Elizabeth Corob
Toby Costin
Double O Charity
Thomas and Simone Fenton
Lindy Fletcher
Michael Frayn
Mr and Mrs Richard Hayden
Mr R Hopkins
Roger Jospe
William Keeling
Lex Service plc
Miss A Lind-Smith
The Mactaggart Third Fund
Fiona McCall
Mrs Nicola McFarlane
Mr J Mills
The Monument Trust
Jimmy Mulville and Denise O'Donoghue
David Murby
Michael Orr
William Poeton CBE and Barbara Poeton
Angela Pullen
Mr and Mrs JA Pye's Charitable Settlement
Ann Scurfield
Ricky Shuttleworth
Brian Smith
The Spotlight
Mr N Trimble
Lionel Wigram Memorial Trust
Madeline Wilks
Richard Wilson
Mrs Katherine Yates

PROGRAMME SUPPORTERS

The Royal Court (English Stage Company Ltd) receives its principal funding from the Arts Council of England. It is also supported financially by a wide range of private companies and public bodies and earns the remainder of its income from the box office and its own trading activities. The Royal Borough of Kensington & Chelsea gives an annual grant to the Royal Court Young Writers' Programme and the London Boroughs Grants Committee provides project funding for a number of play development initiatives.

Royal Court Registered Charity number 231242.

This year the Jerwood Charitable Foundation continues to support new plays by new playwrights with the fifth series of Jerwood New Playwrights.

Since 1993 the A.S.K. Theater Projects of Los Angeles has funded a Playwrights' Programme at the theatre. Bloomberg Mondays, a continuation of the Royal Court's reduced price ticket scheme, is supported by Bloomberg News. This year BSkyB generously committed to a two-year sponsorship of the Royal Court Young Writers' Festival.

FOR THE ROYAL COURT

The Royal National Theatre presents the Market Theatre, Johannesburg production of

THE ISLAND

by Athol Fugard, John Kani and Winston Ntshona

Set in the notorius Robben Island prison, The Island is a tribute to the men and women who, with indomitable courage and a longing for freedom, were imprisoned for taking part in the fight for a free and democratic South Africa.

Following its premiere in 1973, the play toured internationally and was received with enormous acclaim, including Tony Awards for the two actors who are now coming to the National to perform the play for the last time.

In repertoire in the Lyttelton
24 January-26 February
Royal National Theatre
Box Office 0171-452 3000
www.nt-online.org

Funded by THE ARTS COUNCIL OF ENGLAND

DUBLIN CAROL

Characters

JOHN, *late fifties.*

MARK, *early twenties.*

MARY, *thirties.*

The play is set over one day, 24 December:

Part One, *late morning.*

Part Two, *early afternoon.*

Part Three, *late afternoon.*

The action takes place in an office on the Northside of Dublin, around Fairview or the North Strand Road.

This script went to press before the end of rehearsals and may therefore differ from the play as performed at the Royal Court Theatre.

Part One

An office. Dublin. The present.

*The office is furnished with old wooden desks, carpet,
comfortable chairs, filing cabinets, tasteful paintings, elaborate
lamps. But all a bit old and musty. In one corner is a sink with
cups, teapot, kettle, etc. There is an electric fire. There are
terribly scrawny Christmas decorations. A few fairy lights.
A foot high plastic Christmas tree on one of the desks. A little
advent calendar with just a few doors left to open.*

*MARK, a young man of about twenty or twenty-one comes in.
He wears a black suit and an overcoat. He looks a bit wet.
He stands in the office for a few moments by himself, as though
waiting to be told what to do.*

*Then JOHN comes in. He's in his fifties. He also wears a black
suit and overcoat. He's not quite as wet as MARK.*

JOHN. Sorry. I had to make a call. Get your wet gear off,
Mark, yeah?

MARK. Yeah.

JOHN. I'll put the kettle on.

*JOHN fills the kettle. MARK takes his coat off and looks for
somewhere to put it. He drapes it over a chair and stands
with his hands in his pockets.*

JOHN. Plug in that old fire there.

MARK goes down beside a desk and plugs the fire in.

JOHN. You did very well.

MARK. Really?

JOHN. Oh yeah.

*JOHN takes off his coat and takes a hanger from a hook
on the door. He hangs his coat up. He takes a towel from
beside the sink and tosses it to MARK. MARK rubs his hair.*

JOHN. Give your head a rub.

MARK. Thanks Mr. Plunkett.

JOHN. Sit down there.

MARK sits on a chair. JOHN stays near the sink and farts around with the tea. He takes a small bottle of whiskey from a drawer and pours some into a cup.

JOHN. I'm not gonna offer you any of this, son. Your ma'd kill me. I'm old. I'll die if I don't drink this.

MARK (*laughs*). That's alright.

JOHN. I have to have a sup of this.

Pause.

JOHN. You can have a cup of tea in a minute. (*Short pause.*) When the kettle boils up. You know what I mean?

They laugh. (NB: any laughter denoted between the characters need not be literal. Tiny breaths or smiles may suffice and it's up to the actors to find their own rhythm and pitch in rehearsal.)

JOHN. Yeah . . . There's an old pub there across the road, you know? The Strand.

MARK. Yeah I was in there.

JOHN. Yeah?

MARK. Yeah I was in there last night. After work. My girlfriend came down and met me there.

JOHN. Yeah?

MARK. Yeah. She knew it.

JOHN. Yeah?

MARK. Yeah. She knew it from before. She used to work down there in the stationery place.

JOHN. Oh right. Where's she from?

MARK. Marino.

JOHN. Ah well, then, you know?

MARK. Yeah.

JOHN. Up the road.

MARK. Yeah.

JOHN. She's only down the road. A lot of people would know it. Your man does give the regulars a Christmas drink and all this.

MARK. Yeah. It was fairly busy. A lot of people going home from work.

JOHN. Ah yeah, they do a, they used to always do a nice lunch, and you'd get all the people going in there for their nosh. You used to see a lot of priests going in. And that's, did you ever hear that, that's a sign the food is good, you know?

They laugh.

JOHN. Because they know what side their bread is buttered on. That's a little hint for you there now. The old girlfriend, ha? Does she still work up there?

MARK. No she's an air hostess.

JOHN. Oh ho!

MARK *laughs.*

JOHN. Very 'How's it fuckin' goin' . . . '

MARK (*slightly embarrassed*). Yep.

JOHN. The uniform.

MARK. Yep.

JOHN. Did you meet her on a plane?

MARK. Nah. Met her at a party.

JOHN. With the uniform and all.

MARK (*laughs, thinks*). I don't like the uniform.

JOHN. Why?

MARK. I don't know. It makes her legs look fat.

JOHN. Ah now here. Where are you going with that kind of talk? Bloody air hostess, man.

MARK. Well you're going a bit mad about it.

They laugh.

JOHN. I know. What's her name?

MARK. Kim.

JOHN. Kim?

MARK. Yeah.

JOHN. That's eh, that's not an Irish name.

MARK. Mm. I don't know what it is.

JOHN. Is it short for something?

MARK. I don't know.

JOHN. Kipling or . . . Nn. What's she like?

MARK. Em. She's sort of dark. Like her skin is kind of dark.

JOHN. What, sort of tanned or kind of yellowy?

MARK (*laughs*). Yeah kind of.

JOHN. Was she on her holidays?

MARK. No. She just is.

JOHN. Janey Mack. There's people'd love that, you know?

MARK. Yeah.

JOHN. Are you going out long?

MARK. Going out a year and three months.

JOHN. Oh my God. This is the big one, ha?

MARK. You never know.

JOHN. If it's there, it's there, you know? But ah . . . (*Thinks better of what he is going to say.*) . . . you know? How old are you, son?

MARK. Twenty.

JOHN. Jesus. Twenty. God. I don't know. Grasp the nettle. (*Short pause.*) But you obviously don't have any trouble there. In that department.

MARK (*good naturedly*). Give me a break, will you?

JOHN. I'm sorry. Hangover. Has me chatty. You did very well today, do you know that?

MARK. Did I really?

JOHN. Oh yeah. Very good. You're a natural.

MARK *grimaces slightly as if to say 'This better not be my calling.'*

MARK. Do you not find it kind of horrible, though?

JOHN. Ah that person was young, Mark. I'm telling you, it's not usually like that. People get older, they're naturally kind of ready for it, you know? And everybody knows that. And it's all a few quid for the priest and soup and sandwiches in the Addison Lodge. You know? It's different with old people. You get used to it. You were very good. Helping that girl.

MARK (*hoping JOHN agrees*). She couldn't drive.

JOHN (*matter of factly*). No. (*Sly pause.*) What do you reckon? Was she a bit on the side.

MARK (*catching on*). Maybe an old girlfriend or something, alright.

JOHN. He was a drug addict, you know?

MARK. Oh really, yeah?

JOHN. See the amount of fucking young ones? I'd say he was a right little cunt, d'you ever get that feeling? Three and four timing them left right and centre. Did you not see his little missus. Shooting daggers all round the grave?

MARK. Really?

JOHN. It was a mess! (*Short pause.*) Do you think I'm very callous, Mark, yeah?

MARK. No.

JOHN. I often think I must be. But with Noel out sick, and me having to run things a little bit. I've been having a . . . *(Although almost certain of something.)* Are you supposed to just fucking . . .

MARK. Yeah . . . ?

JOHN. No I'm just *(As though this is what he's been wondering about.)* you'd think this kettle would never boil. I don't drink loads of tea. It's a thing with it that people go mad to put the kettle on. I know I'm after putting it on now, but we're wet and so on. But people do be falling all over themselves to be giving you tea all the time.

Distant church bells ring out.

JOHN. Do you go to mass?

MARK. No.

JOHN. The same as meself. Why d'you not go?

MARK. I don't know. It's hard to eh . . . *(Almost unexpectedly deflates.)* Psss. I don't know. I just don't go I suppose.

JOHN. Yeah . . . I haven't gone in years either, you know? Although I feel like I do because there's always mass going on at the funeral. Outside the porch, or sitting in the car like we were today. Go in at the end. Help the poor lads who want to carry the coffin and all this. Nobody carried it today. But you'll get it where they want to. But it should feel like it's a big part of my life because you do always be in churches all the time.

MARK. Well it is, isn't it? Big part of your life. You're more . . . than most people, you know?

JOHN *(slightly vainly, as though they should get the details of his life correct).* I'm *around* it. You know?

MARK. Yeah . . .

JOHN. Are you a Christmas man?

MARK. Yeah, I suppose I am. I like Christmas.

JOHN. Get the little lady a present and so on.

MARK. Well I suppose you have to, don't you? You know?

JOHN. Ah you have to. Get her a nice jumper or something.

They laugh.

MARK. Get her a nice anorak.

JOHN. Oh she'll be delighted. Nice pair of socks in the pockets. Little surprise, you know?

They laugh.

MARK. God. Imagine.

JOHN. Oh there's lads and they do things like that. Buying the wives cutlery and toasters and all sorts of shite. But then again, a lot of it is shite. You know?

They laugh.

JOHN. Fucking hairdriers.

They laugh.

JOHN. You know in the pictures you never see a baldy indian. In the cowboys and indians.

MARK (*thinks*). Yeah.

JOHN. That's you don't wash your hair. You never see a bald knacker. You see the itinerants. They let the natural oils do the business. There's not all hairdriers in the caravans and all this.

MARK. Do you have to get many presents?

JOHN. Ah sure not any more. A boy over in England there, and, you know . . . Jesus I never made you any fucking tea.

JOHN *goes to make tea.*

We can't be having that.

MARK. No, it's fine. I have to go.

JOHN. We never did the advent calendar. You do it.

MARK *goes to the advent calendar and opens a little door on it.* JOHN *makes tea for* MARK.

JOHN. What is it?

MARK. Ahm. It's little angels, like in a choir.

JOHN. A feast of heavenly angels, is it? No it's a host of heavenly angels. 'A feast.' I'm losing the marbles entirely at this stage. Have you gone in to see your Uncle Noel?

MARK. Not yet, no, I haven't. I should go really.

JOHN. Yeah. Ah he's not very well, you know?

MARK. Yeah?

JOHN. Yeah. (*Actively reassuring.*) He'll get better. But just it's not great, in the hospital for Christmas, you know?

MARK. Mmm.

JOHN. But the nurses are great and all that. They help you, you know?

MARK. Yeah.

JOHN. Poor fella. I went in last night. And it was after visiting hours, because of the removal. There was no-one kind of in there. Not even the full lights on and all this. And I think whatever they do to try and have people home at Christmas, there was only one other fella there in the ward. Some auldfella. And he was asleep. And Noelly was there with the telly on, only low, watching some terrible shite altogether. And I was sitting there with him, and he was very tired from all the tests and all this they were doing on him. And it just felt like I should be trying to get him out. Like a jailbreak or something.

They smile.

JOHN. It was all kind of blue, and just the light coming off the telly, (*Ominously.*) on the shiny floor. Aw, it's a different world. You're very helpless. Like the doctors say it's all looking good. But ah . . . Do you know what it was. It was kind of embarrassing. Having to ask if you can do your toilet and all. He had a bit of an upset stomach. From whatever tablets they give him. And instead of asking the nurse for a bit of something, he was lying there and kind of bearing up, you know?

They laugh.

JOHN. And I said, ah, here, I'll lash out to the nurse. Nurse sitting out there on her own at the station. And I go ' Your man in here is feeling a bit yucky, you know?' And she was grand, like. No problem. She gave him this bit of medicine, there, the sad eyes looking up at her. (*Laughs.*) It's terrible, isn't it. Grown up man. Although. Maybe we all like a bit of pampering. What do you think?

MARK (*laughs*). We might. Yeah.

JOHN. Mm. He was great for me. I was very very messy at one time, you know? And he gave me a start here. Got me back into a normal . . . He's a good man. But he will, he'll get out, and he'll be back here. Might give you a bit of a better start here if you want. More permanent. He'll need people.

MARK. Yeah. Well I think I'm gonna try to go to college next year.

JOHN. Oh very good!

MARK. Yeah.

JOHN. Yeah. (*Beat.*) Your mam was saying you were kind of kicking around a bit. No offence.

MARK. No, she's right, you're right. I have been, you know? Been out of school for three years now. And whatever I've been doing. I haven't eh you know.

JOHN. You see, you haven't settled in anywhere.

MARK. Yeah.

JOHN. Well, Jesus, don't worry about it yet, you're only twenty years of age. It's not like you've killed somebody!

They laugh.

JOHN. You'll find your niche. This was mine.

MARK. Is it not any more?

JOHN. Aw no, it is, it has been, I mean. When I found it. And if college isn't starting until next September or whenever it is, you could do a lot worse than this.

MARK. Mm.

JOHN. It can be sad. But there is a dignity to it. (*Short pause.*) Because you're trying to find the dignity. You're trying to afford people a bit of respect in their last little bit with their family and the people around them. Funeral is for the people left behind. That's what it's for. It's not for the dead person. I don't think. Mm. When I go though – very small.

MARK. Yeah?

JOHN. Keeping it all very quiet.

MARK (*with good humoured amusement*). Yeah?

JOHN. Spare people the old hassle.

MARK. But what if people want to pay their respect to you?

JOHN. Ah respect is no use to you when you're gone. If you don't earn it while you're alive, don't be looking for it just because you've happened to die. I never really did any great things. In fact, I've done many things which, to tell you the truth, I'm very very ashamed of. And if you've let people down, don't be wanting them to be all crowding around talking about what a brilliant fella you were, at your funeral, you know? (*With a certain resigned emphatic quality.*) I've seen enough funerals where people have been genuinely heartbroken for me to expect for people to be, you know, mourning me and all this. I just want to slip away, you know? Very quiet. Under cover of darkness.

They give a little laugh.

JOHN. The great escape.

MARK. Yeah. Very morbid.

They laugh.

JOHN. Well. It fucking is. You know?

They laugh.

JOHN. Good Jaysus, these decorations are scaldy.

MARK (*laughs*). They're not the best, alright.

JOHN. I don't know. What do we want? Flashing . . . fairy
lights . . . But of course you know, we have to be a bit cool
because we have so many people in here recently bereaved.
We can't have flashing lights and and Ding Dong Merrily
on High and (*With physicality.*) 'Ah! How's it going?' You
know?

MARK *spits out his tea laughing.*

JOHN. Ah now here. Tea going everywhere and everything
now. God, you get those fellas crooning all bloody
Christmas. It's a real slippers and pipe job. In the rocking
chair. Do you ever see that?

MARK (*a little laugh*). Yeah.

JOHN. Jays, it was great. I used to love all that, you know?
The bloody lengths I used to go to. I was worse than the
kids. Hiding presents all over the place. Leaving out cake
and a drink for Santy. I spent an hour one Christmas eve
telling them Santy didn't like sherry. He liked Macardle's.

They laugh.

Because it was for me, you know? (*Pause.*) Tch. Jaysus. You
know?

Pause.

JOHN. Long time ago now, you know?

Silence. MARK *seems to get ready to go.*

MARK. I better eh . . .

JOHN (*as though stopping him*). D'you want a biscuit, here,
did you have your breakfast?

MARK. I'm grand, I don't really ever eat breakfast.

JOHN. What?

MARK. I have to go anyway. I have to do some stuff.

JOHN (*almost desperately opening a packet of biscuits, offering them to* MARK). Well, you know, you have to . . . you can't be . . . Like I don't care what you do normally. But you're standing out in the cold now. You have to have a bit of fuel in you. Keep you going you know, on your feet all day. In all weathers. Noelly got me in the habit. I used to be like you. I'd nearly be puking if someone put a load of food in front of me in the morning. God, I didn't know how people could do it.

MARK *finally has a biscuit and has to stay a little longer.* JOHN*'s slight hysteria subsides and he relaxes, becoming direct with* MARK.

JOHN. At the same time, I was at a time, in my life, where I was very dependent on drink. D'you understand me?

MARK (*affirmative*). Mm hm.

JOHN. Not that I don't drink now. I still drink. You know? But not in the way that I used to. And the way I was then, Jaysus you'd wake up in the morning and you'd still be very pissed. But horrible. I'm telling you this because this is the story of how I met your Uncle Noel, yeah?

MARK. Yeah, yeah.

JOHN. You'd want to die. All you could do, this'd be the routine, was hang on 'til opening time, in you'd go. One or two lads in the same predicament. The big red faces, and the big swollen fuckin' heads. God the first one or two pints'd knock the fuckin' head off you, but then one or two more, and you'd be feeling a bit better, head home or wherever you call home, you'd probably be able to lie down and get a bit of kip then. Up you'd get, six or seven and off out into the night. Winter nights and summer nights. Winter nights the steam coming off everybodys' wet coats. And the stink of all those dirty bastards leaning into you and snoring in the bar. Summer nights. God, it's amazing what the weather does, nothing's as bad, is it? You'd actually be making the effort. Having a shave and every fucking thing. Clean shirt. Down on the road, waiting on the bus in the summer breeze. Good God. (*Short pause.*)

Now I wasn't always like that and I haven't been like that
since. But this is because of, thanks to Noelly. Bloody
fucking . . . you know, got me. Sorted me out. Got talking
to him in the pub across the road. You know what he's like.
All . . . (*Raises himself up.*) You know, the bearing. You know?

They smile.

MARK. Yeah.

JOHN. He was one of them people. Still is. Always sat there
on his own, reading the paper. Very much his own man, and
keeping himself to himself. But what you'd notice about
him was that he seemed to know everybody. They'd all be
saying hello to him he'd be very much on for a quick chat,
crack a joke or whatever. But then back to himself. Very
much at peace. And one time I asked someone, you know,
who is your man? What does he do? An' when they said,
'Undertaker' you know. It was like. 'Oh right.' That makes
sense. I can see that. And one time, whatever happened,
I was there and there wasn't very many people there and I
was with someone who knew him. This was very civilised
drinking. That's why that was always a great pub. The staff
were very good. Very discreet. Never any messing. I've
been in some terrible fucking places. Filthy dirty places.
Big rows all the time and all. Fucking barman would have a
mattress down behind the bar, fucking be living there and
every fucking thing, you know? I mean, Jesus. But across
the road there, used to be called Hannigan's then. Very
good. And whatever happened this time, there were very
few people there and Noel came in and sat up at the bar like
everyone else and he was chatting away, very dry wit. Had
us all in stitches. And he bought me a drink and I got
chatting to him on his own. He had a great, and he still has
it, a great listening quality, you have it as well.

MARK *smiles a little self-consciously.*

And I was chatting away, this and that and I began to tell
him a bit about myself. Not in any fucking-stupid-pisshead-
very-sorry-for-myself way or anything, anything, like that.
But I explained that I was in a bit of a mess. I had gotten
myself into a terrible mess. This is many years ago. And

I had gone to the stage where I was down to the very last bit of my savings, and I was out of work because I'd basically, no two ways about it, I'd hit the bottle goodo. And I was in and out of my house and I was going to end up on the, the, fucking skids, you know? Be a tramp, you know?

JOHN *is slightly distressed for a second. Just a glimpse of something, a flash in the face.*

It was an extremely bad situation. (*Short pause.*) Now to be fair, I wasn't looking for anything off him. Sure you wouldn't expect for someone to do what he did. I was just basically telling him the truth. And I was generally getting things off my chest. And right there, he says come on back and have a bite and this. Went back, came in here, sat down like where you are and he offers me a job.

You know. Give me a start. And eh . . . God I didn't want to let him down. But your pride kicks in as well. I didn't want to be a charity case on anybody's back. But he sensed that too, you know? And he was able to phrase it properly, more like he needed me more than I needed him, and it was simply a fortuitous thing that had happened – us meeting up. And there was a spare room and all this.

I was so tired. Not just from it being the night-time and everything. But in general. Up he goes and lights a fire in the room. Gives me a pair of pyjamas. What was I like?

They smile.

I was like something out of Peter Pan and Wendy or something. All I needed now was a little Teddy bear.

They laugh.

Jesus. But fair dues. What got me on to this?

Oh yes! Breakfast!

They laugh.

He gets me up in the morning. God. A huge big fry. Rashers and eggs and everything. Pots of tea. Loads of toast. And it got me in the habit. Which is the point I was making.

Mmm.

MARK. What was the job?

JOHN. Same as you today. Carrying wreaths. Lifting out the coffin. And excuse the pun, but generally looking grave. Looking grave and sombre. I'm not a mortician, now, like Noel. There were two other men that were here then. Old Paddy McDermott and Andy Stafford. They're gone now, retired and everything . . . Quiet fellas, you know? And you couldn't bring the subject up . . . But, you see, Noelly would take us all over for a few pints a couple of nights a week. It was like, fucking, like a supervised drink. These were older fellas now. Big lads. Low gruff . . . (*Hunches over.*) . . . voices. And Noelly would buy a few rounds, you know. And I often wondered if, the two boys were . . . if they'd got these jobs in the same way, you know, that I did. Like your Uncle Noel was some . . . He's a very good man, you know?

MARK. Mmm.

JOHN. The more I think about them now. Years on from them. I always remember them as very battered men. They were like they'd had the shit kicked out of them, you know?

MARK is genuinely interested in all of this. His prospects lie ahead of him, and what the world has in store.

JOHN. I think Andy had even been in prison for something. But you'd never ask. But they weren't know-alls like you get in so many pubs in Dublin. God, there's some terrible fucking eejits. The fellas who fucked your ma and forgave your da for letting them. You know?

MARK nearly loses his tea again.

JOHN. Did you never hear that one? Jesus there's some awful men. I'm a Dublin man. Sometimes I wish maybe if I'd lived out in the country, what the hell would I've been like. Probably the same. Bullshit artist.

They smile.

But eh . . . he'd take us over for a pint. But we did see some awful stuff at the same time. Suicides and a woman been killed one time, you know?

MARK. What's the worst thing you've seen?

JOHN. Baby born down a toilet.

MARK. What?!

JOHN. Ah this fucking thing, young girl got pregnant from some fella, some uncle or someone. Course she had no idea what was going on. One because she was fourteen and two because a lot of these people are very stupid and nobody thought there was anything wrong with her. Middle of the night then, she wakes up. In labour. On to the jacks for a few hours. She tried to flush it away but it blocked up the plumbing. I didn't see it down the toilet. I only saw it after.

But ahm . . . And this is the other side of it. I was once over picking up a job in Terenure. This house, wasn't much to look at outside. But inside it was all beautiful. Set back from the road. All the walls knocked in on the inside.

MARK. Open plan.

JOHN. Yes. And big bright airy windows. Very peaceful with the wind going through the leaves out there in the back. And a big long wooden table when we arrived. And a bottle of the hard stuff and a couple of glasses there for us – this was a suicide and the guards had been and it looked all fairly cut and dry. Little old man up in the bed. Tiny wasted away. Sleeping pills and booze there beside the bed. Note and all this. He was, or had been, sick from cancer. And took his own life. Very calm there. Very peaceful. Me and Andy sort of looked down at him in the bed, but we didn't move him for a while. We just sort of went and sat at the big table and stole a nip of the scotch or whatever it was was there. Very relaxed or something. All around were plants and statues of what do you call it? Buddha. (*Pause.*) Mmm. Paddy. Andy. Broken noses and generally battered by life. But never the complaint. Never the fucking moaning Minnie. Unlike my good self. Eejit boy. That's the super-hero I'd be. 'We need to have this fucked up immediately! Quick! Get Eejit Boy!' Who'd you be?

MARK. Horny Man.

They burst out laughing.

JOHN The man with the horn, ha?

MARK. Yeah.

They are quiet for a moment.

JOHN. You might as well be on your way. Come and get your money later.

MARK. Alright.

JOHN. Come in in the afternoon.

MARK. Okay.

JOHN. Good man and well done.

MARK *leaves.*

JOHN *puts the cups on the sink. He goes and puts his own coat on, an anorak. He takes the bottle of whiskey and puts the top on it. He stretches. He unplugs the fire. He coughs.*

JOHN (*absent-mindedly as he leaves*). 'Buddha.'

The lights fade. End of Part One.

Part Two

MARY *comes into the office. She is in her thirties and seems very tired. She looks around a little bit. She then sits.*

JOHN *comes into the office. He carries a bag from the off licence.*

JOHN. I'm sorry. I had to run across the road.

He takes a bottle of whiskey from the bag and opens it. He is dying to get a drink into him.

MARY. You still . . .

JOHN. Oh nowhere near! This is shocking news Mary. And I had to get a few bits for the Christmas. Will you have a drink?

MARY. It's a bit early.

JOHN. Ah Jaysus, shocking news though. For me.

MARY. Just give me a little bit.

JOHN. Yes. I'm glad. Not drinking on my own.

JOHN *gives them both a drink of neat whiskey in old mugs.* JOHN *shoots his back in one, his eyes nearly coming out on stalks. He immediately pours himself another.* MARY *takes a sip from hers. It's too strong for her.*

MARY. Can I have a drop of water?

JOHN. Oh yes, of course.

He takes her drink over to the sink and pours some water in.

JOHN. We're really closed but I have to give a youngfella his wages later. So handier here.

MARY. That's fine.

JOHN. This is terrible news. I'll have to sort out going in.

MARY. Oh you *have* to . . . ?

JOHN. Well I should I think. I think I should.

MARY. Of course you should! What are you talking about?

JOHN. I'm just saying I have to go in.

MARY. Of course you have to.

JOHN. What's wrong?

MARY. Just you make it like such a chore. For you.

JOHN. No. Just I've been in and out seeing Noel, the man who runs this business. And it's just. Going to the hospital. I don't know. I didn't mean anything.

MARY (*softens a little*). Come with me today.

JOHN. What time are you going in at?

MARY. I could pick you up at five or something. (*Pause.*) Okay?

JOHN (*awkward, guarded*). Is Paul gonna come home?

MARY. He's coming on Monday.

JOHN. How is he, alright, yeah?

MARY. The same as me, just can't believe it.

JOHN. But in general.

MARY. He fixes motorbikes, with this friend of his.

JOHN. English fella.

MARY. Yeah.

JOHN. What, like you go over?

MARY. I just been twice. I was there in the summer.

JOHN. But he's alright.

MARY. Yeah he's . . . He's the same as he was. Drifts along. He's getting like you though, more and more.

JOHN. Yeah? God.

A slightly awkward moment passes between them which MARY *breaks, just for something to say.* *

MARY. I don't know if I could live there.

JOHN. Yeah?

MARY (**direct, almost without expression*). It's like Coronation Street. That's what it's like. That's what it looks like.

JOHN. Yeah?

MARY. The little streets. All little terraced houses and all. Up and down these hills. When I was there. Every day it was you go around the corner and either get a pizza or an Indian or a Chinese.

JOHN. Out of the take-away.

MARY (*regaining expression and lucidity*). Yeah. Yeah. Just do that all the time. His friend Craig comes around and they stand in this little back garden drinking beer and tinkering around with motorbikes. I used to go and sit in this graveyard.

JOHN. How is he getting like me?

MARY. The way he says things and nods. The way he stands in the pub and things like that.

JOHN. And what do yous say? About me and all that?

MARY. He doesn't . . . He doesn't say anything. About you.

JOHN *exhales deeply.*

MARY. You look much older.

JOHN. Yeah?

MARY *nods.*

JOHN. I am older, you know? D'you want another drink?

MARY. No.

JOHN *pours himself one.*

JOHN. Little smartener.

MARY. Yeah. (*Again softens a little, brings* JOHN *in . . .*) He has this horrible girlfriend.

JOHN. Yeah?

MARY. Yeah well she's not really any more. But she doesn't leave him alone. She's a little scrawny thing. Her hair is in bits. And she has terrible acne because she only eats pub grub and chocolate. She's like a little monkey. She gets pissed and comes round to his house. It was very funny. She came around one day and we had to lie down in the living room near the wall so she couldn't see us. Me and Paul and Craig. God, it was hard not make any noise, I was bursting out laughing. I thought I was going to wet myself. She was there for ages. One of the neighbours even came out and asked her what was wrong with her. God it was awful. She's a bit mad, like, I think.

JOHN. Tch.

They look at each other.

MARY. She caught us in one night. It was so hot we had the front door open. Because there's no hall, just the front room where we were sitting. In she walks. It was awful. She plonked herself down and started just talking. It was so weird. She wouldn't go. I just went up to bed. But she was there in the morning. She only went when me and Paul pretended to go out.

JOHN (*a little laugh*). Mmmm.

Pause.

MARY. Mmm.

JOHN. How are you doing? I'm sorry, this is very hard.

MARY. Yeah, I'm . . . I'm working in Dunnes. In Stephen's Green.

JOHN. Oh right. Okay.

MARY. It's alright, you know. It's okay.

JOHN. Well that's alright, isn't it?

MARY (*looks around, no pause*). I'll have to do all this . . . funeral . . .

Silence.

JOHN. What else are you doing?

MARY. I don't know. Sometimes I drive down the country. Wonder what the fuck I'm doing there and come back.

JOHN. You remember down in Limerick. Where we used to go.

MARY. Yeah. When Paul lost his shoes.

JOHN. Oh God yeah. Jesus. The ructions.

MARY. Mmm.

JOHN. We had some great times down there. You might have been too young.

MARY. No I remember. I remember Paul losing his shoes. I remember standing in the middle of a load of nettles one time. Couldn't go anywhere without being stung. Just standing there in this little sleeveless dress I loved. Getting stung to bits. You came in through the nettles and lifted me out.

JOHN. Yeah.

MARY. I remember one night. We were all in the house and you hadn't come home. Auntie Rita wanted Mam to ring the guards. Or ring the hospitals to see what had happened. But Mam knew you'd come back.

JOHN. I was gone to the pictures.

MARY. What?!

JOHN. I mean first.

MARY. Yeah, not all night.

JOHN. Yeah I went to the pub.

MARY. Oh Duh . . .

JOHN. Yeah well that's where I was.

MARY. Course you were.

JOHN. I used to get caught down the country. Up home they kick you out at eleven. But you'd be chancing a quick one like that, those boys'll (*i.e., barmen in the country*) serve you 'til two o'clock in the morning. So you'd think you were catching them for a quick one after the pictures. But the door'd be locked and it was just getting going.

MARY. Do you know how many years it is, since I've seen you?

JOHN. I don't know.

MARY. That day I met you on Henry Street and we went for a cup of coffee.

JOHN. Oh yeah . . . ?

MARY. That's ten years ago.

JOHN. Okay.

MARY. And you're still, you're still making bloody excuses about a night in Limerick, what twenty-five years, ago. I just, I don't believe it.

JOHN. Well, I'm telling you.

MARY. I know. But. Here I am. I don't know what to call you. Our lives are . . .

JOHN. It happens a lot.

MARY (*marvelling at him*). But you're still, here making excuses.

JOHN. But what do you want me to say?

MARY. I don't know. But it's like you're treating me like a fool. 'I'd get caught . . . A quick one after the pictures . . . ' If you even went to the pictures. When Mam was in hospital having Paul I remember Auntie Rita came to stay. You slept in with me. And you had a bottle of something up in the wardrobe. I woke up and you were sitting down against the radiator.

JOHN. I couldn't sleep.

MARY. See again, there's an excuse.

JOHN. Of course there's an excuse. You think I'd deliberately want to hurt you? I wish it was different. But that's what I needed to do.

MARY. Yeah but do you not . . . (*The rest is unspeakable.*)

Silence. JOHN explodes.

JOHN. What do you want me to say about it? I'm not going to just say, 'I'm sorry' – because of the fucking enormity of all the fucking things I did. It's not enough. Jesus. I know. I know. I think about everybody. You're telling me Helen is going to die?! Where am I supposed to be? I remember her years ago. Jesus, how can I go and look at that? Should I, even?

MARY. You're her husband.

JOHN. I'm not her fucking husband! What kind of fucking husband am I? That's all gone.

MARY. It'd mean a lot to her.

Pause.

JOHN. She wants me to go?

MARY *nods.* JOHN *closes his eyes and hangs his head.*

JOHN. Tch.

He makes a long hissing sigh.

JOHN. What goes through people's minds? (*Short pause.*) Is she in a state, like?

MARY. No she's exhausted just. You'd want to see her if it was you.

JOHN. No I wouldn't. I'd want it all over quick as possible.

MARY. No I don't believe that.

JOHN (*tone of 'That's your opinion'*). Well.

MARY. I'd want to see you.

Pause.

JOHN. Why?

Pause.

MARY. Because I love you.

Long pause.

JOHN. Why do you love me?

MARY. I can't help it. I always think about you. And I . . . (*Matter-of-factly.*) I hate you too.

JOHN. I think about you as well, you know? Don't do this.

Pause.

MARY. I had this boyfriend. He wasn't my boyfriend. I don't know what I was thinking. He was, this friend of mine at work, he was her brother. He was a big . . . they're from Kildare. He was a big culchie, teacher. Primary school

teacher. I met him when we were out one night. There's this
place, Major Tom's. I was. I just wanted something to
happen. He was there. A big shiny red face. I didn't . . .
I wasn't serious about him. I saw him a few times. Drinking
stupid cocktails around those places up there around the
centre. And I just came up the steps with him one night,
into the street. And whatever it was, the way the buildings
looked, it took me back in time. And I felt that, you . . .
I felt that you were with me. And this guy Ger, he was
always pissed. He wanted me to go back to his house with
him. And I know this is weird, but it was like he was,
compared to you, even as a messer, compared to you, he
was such a fucking amateur.

They give a little laugh.

MARY. Do you know? That even in the morning all he'd
complain about would be his hangover and how he had
copybooks to correct. Where you'd be looking for money to
hit the bottle . . .

JOHN. Which is terrible . . .

They are smiling a little, JOHN *shaking his head.*

JOHN. For who I was and who you were and what I should
have been looking for money for.

MARY. Sometimes I smell you. Everything comes back.

JOHN. I know.

MARY. I can smell it now.

JOHN. It's Brut.

Pause.

MARY. Do you still see . . . Carol . . . ?

JOHN. Oh, no. I don't even want to talk about it.

MARY. I know she didn't take you away. I know she looked
after you.

JOHN. She kept me going. She liked me too much. Warts and
all. Horrible characteristics and everything. That was the

problem. Would've watched me kill myself if that was what I wanted.

MARY. I remember the weekend you left.

JOHN. Don't . . .

MARY. It was a Friday, you came to collect me from school. And it was usually Mam and I came out and whatever was going on, it was you instead of her. And I remember you could hardly stand without swaying. You were hanging on to the railings and we went to get the bus. And the smell of drink off you.

JOHN. I know.

MARY. And you didn't know what the hell you were doing, and we went and got the bus on the wrong side of the road.

JOHN. This is all a long time ago.

MARY. And we went into town! And you couldn't talk properly or anything.

JOHN. I know.

MARY. Jesus. Neither of us knew where the hell we were. I was only seven. And you must've been drinking for days.

JOHN. I know.

MARY. And you took me into a pub! I don't know how you managed to, but you got a drink. I don't think the barman saw me. You were up on a stool. I was down on the ground and all I could do was take out my school books. I remember looking at my religion book and wanting Jesus to come and get me. You were like somebody else.

JOHN. I know.

MARY. There was a row or something and you fell on top of me.

JOHN. This is awful.

MARY. A ban guard took me home.

JOHN. I know. Terrible things happen. You have a temper and you're not talking to someone. And you calm down and try to keep your heart, fucking, somehow open. But you go and hit the fucking bottle. And you make everything fucking worse. I know you want me to say I'm sorry.

MARY. No . . .

JOHN (*although calm, he is trawling a black place*). But I can hardly remember anything. I was in a very bad state. I don't want to make any excuses, but Jesus Christ! I was in hell. I was in agony. And nobody knew. And I didn't know what to do about it. You don't know. I am sorry. I am sorry. I'm sorry about the whole stinking business. I think about it now and I want to puke. I wish I'd never been born. It's all been awful.

MARY. No. It hasn't all been awful.

JOHN. No. It's been awful for me and I made it terrible for you and your mother and Paul. God. There was one morning I was with Carol, down there in her house, down there in Sybil Hill. And whatever was wrong with me, I was after getting out of bed. I was in bed with this woman, Mary! You were in school. And I went over to the window. She had these venetian blinds with tassles on the end of them. And it was these tassles. I was looking out at her bit of a garden there and these tassles. Tassles on the blinds. And whatever it was, I knew I'd fucking blown it, you know? Because although I'd never would've given a flying shite about blinds and tassles on them it was just something your mother would never have bought. Because it was crummy. It was gaudy or whatever. And I suddenly felt like I was miles and miles away from you and Helen and Pauly. And I knew I couldn't go back. Because I was dirty. I was a dirty filthy dirty man. And you're making me think about it. I'm often wondering where Pauly is. Over in England and all. And if he's thinking about me. God I feel like my brain is going to burst. And you come in and you're so like your mother, and I often, just sometimes wish you'd just fuck off.

MARY. I know.

JOHN. There was this day. I woke up in Carol's house, sick and everything all over my clothes. And I took some of her husband's clothes. She kept them! Oh it was awful. She kept them for all those years. He'd been dead longer than they'd been married. It was like a nightmare. And I put on his gear and started walking home. Hoping to God, for once that your mother would be there! I was changing everything. I needed her to be there. I was going to change it all and get help and basically apologise to everybody. And there I was coming down the road, and I saw her face at the window, looking out, and I was going 'Yes!' 'It's all over, I'll never go this low again . . . ' And I got in the door and went to where she was there, but it wasn't her, it was the breadboard or something there against the window. So. Do you know what I did?

MARY. I can guess.

JOHN. Yeah, off out on another bender. In a dead man's clothes? 'I'll never go this low?' I'd managed to go even further.

Short pause.

I knew when it was happening. At the beginning. There was a lot of money knocking about in those days. And a lot of parties. And if I had second sight or something. I knew I was absolutely fucked. Be there in someone's new house at Christmas. People all enjoying themselves, all the fucking wives expecting babies. And it was like I could see the soul of the party or something. The kick off the first few drinks. Like the soul of the party was like a beautiful girl dancing through the room. And then, of course by the end of the night when I'd basically insulted and alienated everyone, the soul of the party was this old fucking cripple that didn't even have the energy to complain or ask for help any more. Me leaving those places, the fucking silence behind me as I left was . . . fucking . . . deafening.

MARY. I'm not . . . I didn't come here to hurt you.

JOHN. What do you mean?

MARY. I don't know. I feel like I'm hurting you.

JOHN. You can't hurt me. What have I done? (*Short pause. He's trying to express that she seems very real to him all of a sudden.*) You know? I'm looking at you. I'm looking at you there, you know?

MARY. Do you want me to go? I don't want to go.

JOHN (*he's belting back the whiskey*). Oh fucking hell.

MARY. Do you . . . ever wish you could . . . go back and have it all different?

JOHN. Go back? No way. I just wish it never happened I don't want anything to exist, you know? Of what happened.

MARY. You don't want me to exist?

JOHN. Not like this! Not with me as your . . . dad.

MARY (*matter of factly, no malice*). I'm not happy. (*Either.*)

JOHN. I know. Don't! This is horrible.

MARY. But I don't know if it's your fault. I'm kind of an eejit, as well on my own, like, you know?

Pause. They laugh.

MARY. You know?

JOHN. You're an eejit in your own right . . .

MARY (*a little laugh*). Yeah.

JOHN. Oh God . . . Well I know where you got it.

MARY. What was Mum like?

JOHN *pours them more drink.*

JOHN. I don't know. I don't know. Quiet. Embarrassed. This is mad. I always felt sorry for her.

MARY. Is that why you were with her?

JOHN. Maybe. I was always sort of fucking perverse. You know? Doing things for the sheer hell of it. Doing stupid things just to sort of see what'd happen.

MARY. Were you just pretending. To love her?

JOHN. I don't know. No. Love . . . What the fuck is that, you know. Ah you just generally get into a sort of a routine. Just . . . Are you . . . se close?

MARY. Yeah.

MARY *starts crying.*

MARY. Sorry.

She gets a tissue from her bag, wiping her nose.

MARY. I'm just thinking about her.

Pause.

MARY. You know, whatever kind of happened to her, because of you and all that. It, whatever way, she had a great strength or something, because of it.

JOHN. Okay.

MARY. There was humour, even, you know?

JOHN. Yeah.

MARY. I'm talking about her in the past already.

JOHN. Well that's . . . you know, you want to get it over with.

MARY. I know I love her, you know?

JOHN. You're full of fucking loving everybody today and all that. Yeah?

MARY (*gently*). You're horrible. Were you always this horrible?

JOHN. I don't mean it.

MARY. She was very lenient and all, you know? On Paul. God, he was a handful. The guards were looking for him and everything, you know?

JOHN. For what?

MARY. Ah he told some ban guard to go fuck herself. In town somewhere.

JOHN. What happened?

MARY. Ah I don't know. She told him to be quiet coming out of a pub or something.

JOHN. Is he a fucking eeejit, is he?

MARY. No! He's great. But I remember Mum sitting at the kitchen table laughing. and lighting up a fag. And I remember thinking about her. Right then. And knowing that I loved her. Right in that moment. That's how I know. And I was thinking about you. And I was thinking that you'd be really good friends. And it was sort of a pity or something that you were a man and a woman, you know. Like if you could have both been men, or both been women. I don't know. I just remember that, you know?

JOHN. Or if we were just bloody older. You know? Or maybe being older doesn't even make any difference. You just have to be good, don't you? That's the thing. The man who owns this business was very good to me. I've never been good to anybody. There's something I can't help it. I needed like a teacher or something. The man who runs this business, Noel, he's in hospital having tests done, right? And he's such a kind and a, a, a good person. He doesn't deserve to be sick, nobody does, you know? But there I was, visiting him there. And do you know what was going through my mind? I was going, part of me was, it was like a little tune, I didn't know what it was until I listened to it. I was thinking, 'Here you are all tucked up in hospital, all fucking not well and all this. And I'm up and about, bullshitting for Ireland, rapping along with barmen, and you never hurt a fly. But you're a stupid cunt, because you're sick. You're a wanker, because you're all weak and sick there, taking your medicine.' I felt like I hated him because the poor bastard isn't well. You see, that's mean. That's what I have.

MARY. I don't think that matters. I . . . I don't care.

JOHN. Well I blow my own fucking mind.

MARY. You were sick too. You were sick in your head.

JOHN. I was just sick of my fucking self.

MARY. But that's . . . that's the same.

JOHN (*slightly dismissive*). Yeah, yeah.

MARY (*as though wanting to prove she is like him*). Everybody hated me.

JOHN. What do you mean?

MARY. I was a weird girl.

JOHN. No you weren't.

MARY. When I got older. You'd see me walking around the estate on my own, walking the dog and having a smoke.

JOHN. What dog?

MARY. We got a dog. Snoopy.

JOHN. Really? It's like I feel like I have a dog now.

MARY. He's dead.

JOHN. Okay.

MARY. People used to say that girl's not right.

JOHN. People are only stupid. Ganging up on you.

MARY. I didn't care. I liked it. It made me feel like I was closer to you because I was sort of like you.

JOHN (*shakes his head slowly*). Em.

MARY (*reading him*). But I was only playing at it.

JOHN. You didn't destroy your life. But someone saved me. You know?

MARY. I think that's what I was looking for.

JOHN. You don't need it.

Pause.

MARY. What *happened* to you?

Pause.

JOHN. Boredom. Loneliness. A feeling of basically being out of step with everybody else. Fear. Anxiety. Tension. And of course, a disposition to generally liking the whole fucking thing of drinking until you pass out.

MARY. But what were you worried about?

Pause.

JOHN. I just always felt like people were judging me. I just always felt guilty.

MARY. Why?

JOHN. I don't know. Why do all these young . . . drug addicts . . . I see people my generation. You see them there in their suit jackets. Sitting on some street corner. Begging for money for drink. You think they don't know it's a short term solution? They know. But the long term is terrifying. Failure reaching up and grabbing you. We were brought up like that a little bit. You know? That we were all going to hell or somewhere. You know?

Short pause.

My dad used to beat the living daylights out of my mother, you know? (*Pause.*) He used used to come in and hammer the fucking head off her. Tusssss. And you're only a young boy. You're fucking hiding under the bed, you'd hear him come in roaring. And . . . It wasn't that I was going, 'I'm too young to do anything.' It was something else. I was just . . . shit scared. And I let her take it. So he wouldn't hit me. That feeling went away, when I got older. He became a little frail old man and stopped all that shennanigans. And I fucking just generally forgot about it, you know? But then, years later, when you were born, right? I started to feel again like I was a . . . coward. Do you see I thought the world was a bad place and that someone was going to come and attack us.

MARY. Who?

JOHN. I don't know. But somewhere in me. I knew . . . I'd let you . . . and your mammy . . . down. That if we were attacked. I knew deep down in me, that I'd run away and leave yous to it. You a little baby. And your mother like a little squirrel or something.

MARY. No-one was going to attack us.

JOHN. I knew that! But this was a thing that I couldn't help feeling. And it was a terrible fucking feeling to have. And I just believed in it. And I sort of, let yous all down, just *to get it over with*. Or something.

Pause.

JOHN. I don't understand it.

Pause.

MARY. You could do her funeral.

JOHN. Oh No! No! Mary, no!

MARY. Is that . . .

JOHN. Aw God, Jesus, no . . .

MARY. That's . . . yeah?

JOHN. I couldn't.

MARY. I know.

JOHN. Bad enough, seeing her, but putting her down, in the muck, for fuck's sake Mary.

MARY. Okay.

JOHN. Yeah. There in her dressing gown?! A man in his pyjamas is bad enough. But a woman there in her nightdress. Very much a lady and not a man. And the betrayal and the guilt and everything written all over our fucking faces.

MARY. Don't drink any more.

JOHN. What?

MARY. Don't drink any more before you see her. Be sober, alright?

JOHN. I am sober.

MARY. Yeah but don't drink any more. (*She becomes upset.*) Please.

JOHN (*aggravated*). Okay. Alright. Jesus.

MARY. I'm sorry.

JOHN. No. Oh God!

MARY. Don't see her if . . . you can't.

JOHN (*inhales deeply*). Oh Mary.

MARY. I'll say I couldn't see you or . . .

> JOHN *puts his hand to his face.*

MARY. Okay? (*Short pause.*) I'll tell her I couldn't find you.

JOHN (*exhales*). No.

MARY. I'll help you. We'll go together.

> *She wants to go near him. But stays where she is.*

MARY. Dad.

> JOHN *looks at her.*

MARY. I'll help you. I'll be with you.

JOHN (*accepting*). Yeah. (*Beat.*) Yeah.

> *There's a long pause. In which neither know what to say.*

MARY. I'll call here at five.

JOHN. Okay.

MARY (*as much to convince herself as him*). It'll be alright. It'll be alright.

JOHN. I . . . want to make it up to you.

MARY. Nnn . . . (*Unable to take any more.*) I'm gonna call back at five. Okay, Dad?

JOHN. I'll be here.

> *She stays for a moment. And then leaves.* JOHN *stands there.*

> *The lights fade. End of Part Two.*

Part Three

We hear the bells chiming. Four o'clock. JOHN is slumped in a chair. Three quarters of the whiskey is gone. He sleeps in a drunken stupor. There is a soft knocking at the door.

MARK (*off*). Mr. Plunkett?

> MARK *opens the door and steps in. He is in casual gear now, and consequently looks younger.*

MARK. Mr. Plunkett?

> JOHN *is startled.*

JOHN. What? Paul?

MARK. It's Mark.

JOHN. What are you doing? I haven't gone to the bank.

MARK. Oh. Okay.

JOHN. What time is it?

MARK. Are you alright?

JOHN. Have I missed the bank? What time is it?

MARK. It's five past four.

JOHN. Bollocks. Ah for fuck's sake. I'm sorry.

> JOHN *fishes into his pockets.*

JOHN. Are you waiting on it? How much are you owed?

MARK. Forget about it.

JOHN. Ah for fuck's sake, I'm sorry. Here. What's this?

> JOHN *counts some money out of his pocket. It's all different notes bundled in little balls.*

JOHN. I'm just, I'm sorry, I've had a horrible . . . What's this? Look there's thirty . . . five . . . Ah I'm sorry.

MARK. Ah it's okay.

JOHN. Will that do you?

MARK. Ah yeah, no, that's grand.

JOHN. I have to go.

JOHN *tries to get his coat. He knocks some furniture over,* MARK *helps him.*

MARK. Are you okay?

JOHN. I need the toilet.

MARK *gets him to the toilet.*

JOHN. Will you put the kettle on?

MARK. Yeah. Sure.

JOHN *goes into the toilet.* MARK *puts water in the kettle and turns it on.*

He then stands there, leaning, lost in thought.

JOHN *reappears, wiping his mouth with some tissue. He watches* MARK. MARK *doesn't notice him.*

JOHN. Are you alright?

MARK (*snapping out of it*). Yeah. Are you okay?

JOHN. Yeah, I just. I had a good bit to drink. (*Realising* MARK*'s demeanour.*) Have you had a few?

MARK. I've had a couple.

JOHN *watches* MARK *making the tea.*

JOHN. You're not very full of Christmas cheer.

MARK *acknowledges this. A snort.*

JOHN. Do you want a drink?

MARK. Is that alright?

JOHN. Of course it is! Christmas eve!

MARK. Thanks.

MARK *pours himself a drink.*

MARK. Do you want one?

JOHN. Oh Jesus, just give me a small one. Just put a drop in my tea.

MARK *pours a drink for* JOHN *and hands it to him.*

JOHN. Thanks.

MARK *takes a large slug of whiskey. He doesn't seem used to it.*

JOHN. Are you alright?

MARK.Yeah.

JOHN. Do you want to maybe put some water in that?

MARK. No, it's okay.

MARK *takes another large slug.*

JOHN. Are you annoyed with me or something?

MARK. What?

JOHN. Are you annoyed at me about your money?

MARK. Ah, no. No.

JOHN. What's wrong with you?

MARK. Nothing. I just didn't have a . . . brilliant afternoon. I'm fine.

JOHN. What happened?

MARK. Nothing.

Pause.

JOHN. Okay.

MARK. Just. When I left here I was going to do something. And I didn't do it, you know?

JOHN. What is it? Do you want me to do it for you?

MARK (*a little laugh*). No. Eh . . . you know Kim. I was telling you . . . earlier.

JOHN. Don't tell me you didn't get her something.

MARK. No. No, no, no.

Pause.

JOHN: What's wrong?

MARK. I just went down to break it off with her, you know?

JOHN. On . . . Christmas eve?

MARK. No. It's just, she's all on for us to go away together next week. You know? And I don't want to just be making excuses. So I . . . I know it's not a great time. But you know, she's become . . . very intense. About me. And I'm not . . . you know the same.

JOHN. You're not the same about her.

MARK. No.

JOHN.Tch. So you toddled off to tell her.

MARK *nods.*

JOHN. Down in Marino.

MARK. Yeah.

Pause.

MARK. She'd been in work. She started at six or four this morning or something. She was knackered. And I went in to tell her. To her gaff. Her ma let me go up. She was having a lie down.

JOHN (*gives a little laugh*). This is not brilliant.

MARK. I know.

JOHN. What did you say?

MARK (*pause*). Mr. Plunkett. (*Beat.*) I don't know. I just was blurting away there. Just her face . . . Just this really faint high-pitched noise started to come out of her.

JOHN. It just couldn't have gone worse. I know. Don't worry about it.

MARK. No . . .

JOHN. She probably has some serious mental disability or something.

MARK. She started sort of grabbing me. And this . . . noise. I was, here, it's okay, it's okay.

JOHN *snorts.*

MARK. I thought that like if she was my sister or something. I just stayed there with her. Like no-one should . . . (*Cause this much hurt.*) I basically told her I didn't mean it. I've been on my own in the pub across the road for two hours.

MARK *looks at* JOHN.

JOHN. Mm. Well, you know, it might look like you made a bollocks of it.

MARK. Well that's what it feels like.

JOHN. Yeah, but she might've been pulling a sneaky on you, you know?

MARK. No this was, this was real man.

JOHN. Here, give us a drop of that. Give yourself a lash. (*Looks around sharply.*) What time is it?

MARK *pours them both some whiskey.*

JOHN. Okay, it was real. She had a genuine freak attack, but there's an element of blackmail, in that, do you know what I mean?

Pause.

MARK. That she did it on purpose?

JOHN. She mightn't have done it completely on purpose, but when she felt it coming on, you know? She let the fucking thing fly. You know?

MARK *laughs.*

JOHN. I'm telling you. You wouldn't be up to them.

MARK. Ah I don't think she'd . . . you know?

JOHN. Yeah but look at it now. Here's you all fretting. You're getting all limbered up to go on a fucking bender. All

fucking despair and moaning to your mates on Christmas
eve, all tomorrow wondering if she's gonna eat a bottle
of tablets, or end up in Grangegorman, you know? And
where's she? She's tucked up in bed, with her mammy
filling her full of cup-a-soup and talking about watching
Raiders of the Lost Ark later on and pulling the couch over
to the fire and eating chocolate liquers. Do you see what
I mean?

MARK (*laughs*). I just don't think it was on purpose.

JOHN. Look you had a difficult thing to do. You were going
down there to tell her the truth. And it was gonna be hard,
because I can see by you that you're a sensitive kind of
chap, and you were concerned about her feelings. You aren't
in the business of dishing out pain and agony and not giving
a bollocks. So there you are trying to give the whole thing a
bit of respect. It's not like you were doing a bunk with some
black girl or hopping on the next train to Timbuctoo. You
did the hard thing. And what does she do?

MARK. She might have been still kind of asleep or something
though.

JOHN. Yeah but you're upset as well, but you're engaging in it
in a grown-up way of sitting down and talking about it. We
can all throw fits. We can all lose the head. But that's
selfish, though, as well. Because it's mean. It's 'Fuck you.
I'm not talking to you.' No acknowledgement that you're
trying to do the right thing or nothing, none of that. Just
basically, 'Ah you've driven me into the grave, and now
you're cursed by the gypsies of County Carlow,' you know?
It's bollocks.

Pause.

MARK. I should ring her.

JOHN. Nah! Let her ring you. She's probably fucking stalking
you now, anyway. She's probably across the road with a
pitchfork.

MARK *gives a little laugh.*

JOHN. Anyway. That's dangerous love. It's different kinds of love that men and women give. A woman's love can be terribly constant. Good God. It can last for years! (*Pause.*) There was this woman loved me unconditionally for many years. Gave me lifts everywhere. Waited for me. And waited for me in the long term as well. Waiting on me . . . She was a widow, you know? And I was still married. I was going into a nose dive on the booze. It had a real hold of me. She was very very lonely. Living in a house up there in Sybil Hill. She was holding down this part time job. Not much money. She had a little Fiat 127.

She used to drink pots of tea up there in The Beachcomber in Killester up there. And I'd be skiving off work early, sneaking around pubs all up in Raheny and Killester and Harmonstown and then all down here and into town.

Got chatting to her in The Beachcomber. And she hooked me because she could see that I was very taken with getting bollocksed and she'd buy me drinks. And it got that I'd . . . I'd rely on her being in there. This is mad, you know? And then it was whiskey up in the gaff. (*Pause.*) And I followed the trail of breadcrumbs all the way into bed. I was more into the drink than the sex though. She was into neither. She just couldn't take it on her own. Being on her own. So there we were. Her loving me and me treating it like a convenience.

I thought of it like God had sent me like a drink-angel. Like I believed in God and he'd sent this to take care of me. And that she was like all confused because she didn't know why God had sent her. And she didn't know why she loved me but she just did. God I used to feel sorry for her. Giving me her last bit of money. Giving me her last fiver and me asking her if she didn't have any more?! Counting out her change trying to get it up to the four pints! But that was the awful disservice I was doing her. The vanity. No it wasn't vanity. Just that I'd been taught to believe in God! Poor stupid bitch. You have no idea. You have no idea.

But that was it. I had somewhere to go where I'd get bollocksed and blot out that I had a, a, a fucking life

somewhere else. So it was easy. And that's dangerous love.
That unconditional, 'I'll do anything to keep you,' fucking
thing. God she had me pickled. You're well shot of this one
and that's the end of it. What are you going to do? Basically
torture yourself until you feel better? You won't feel better
so just . . . bollocks.

Pause.

MARK. Mm.

JOHN. Yeah.

MARK *pours himself a nip of whiskey and pours some into*
JOHN's *mug.*

MARK. But that's like a fit as well.

JOHN. What?

MARK. You baling off, on your family.

JOHN (*considers*). I'm in a fog.

MARK. Like, you're saying about Kim, that she threw a
    freaker and that's . . . not fair on me.

JOHN (*vaguely affirmative*). Uhh.

MARK. You doing a bunk. How is that . . . facing . . . up . . .

JOHN. Well, that's how I know what I'm talking about.

MARK. That's bollocks.

JOHN. What am I supposed to do? Stand here and defend
    myself all day?

MARK. Well then don't be dispensing fucking . . . wisdom . . .
    I feel like a fucking asshole! You're here telling me what to
    do? (*Fiercely.*) I just feel like a fucking eejit!

JOHN. I'm only trying to help you! Why don't you let me
    finish?! I'm like the opposite of you . . . What? Am I talking
    to you like you're a kid? Is that it?

Pause.

JOHN. What do you want?

MARK. I'm, look, I'll see you later.

MARK starts to go.

JOHN. Don't go like this Mark. It's Christmas.

MARK. Fuck off.

MARK is leaving.

JOHN. My wife is dying. I need someone I can talk to, son.

MARK. What?

JOHN. She has cancer in her neck.

Pause.

MARK. This is your wife?

JOHN. Yeah. I haven't seen her for eh, for many years now, you know?

MARK. I'm sorry . . . to hear that.

JOHN. Yeah, well. You know, it's not something I should eh, I should be sympathised with about really. You know?

Silence.

JOHN. They want me to do her funeral.

Long pause.

JOHN. What do you think?

MARK. I . . . don't know . . .

JOHN. You're right, you know? About me.

MARK. Look. I don't . . .

JOHN (*slightly too bossy*). Listen to me! (*Apologetic.*) I'm sorry. No. Listen. Listen to me. I'm sorry.

MARK. It's okay. It's alright.

JOHN. My daughter's coming. I don't have much time. She wants me to go to the hospital and see her. I'm just, I really don't know what to do. Your Uncle Noel would know.

Short pause.

MARK. You should go.

JOHN. Yeah?

MARK. You . . . probably should. What if you don't . . . And she . . .

Pause.

JOHN. No. No, you're right. (*Pause. Facing a terrible prospect.*) Paul, he's my . . . son, you know? He's coming home from England. And I haven't seen him since he was eh . . . (*Pause.*) He came around here one time a few years ago. Looking for me. (*He screws up his face a little.*) And I said I wasn't here, you know? They told him I wasn't here. And I just sat over there, waiting until he was gone. And then I changed my mind and went out after him. I just kept going up and down the North Strand looking for him. But, he was gone obviously and that was all there was about it. But I got a letter from him a bit later, telling me he got his Leaving Cert. This is a few years ago. Yeah. What time is it?

MARK. Half four.

JOHN. I better drink some tea.

JOHN begins to get up.

MARK. I'll get it.

JOHN sniffs.

JOHN. Thanks. Here, you might as well do the advent calendar. We won't be here tomorrow.

MARK gives a little laugh.

MARK. Okay.

JOHN. Have a little thrill. Knock yourself out.

MARK laughs. He opens the last door on the advent calendar.

JOHN. What is it?

MARK. It's Jesus.

JOHN. Of course it is. Will you do something for me?

MARK. Yeah.

JOHN. There should be an old box out there in the yard. I want to get the decorations down.

MARK *goes to the door and comes back with a box.*

MARK. I'll give you a hand.

MARK *begins taking things down.*

JOHN. There's nothing worse than decorations after Christmas. That's the way I sometimes used to feel putting my clothes on in the morning.

JOHN *starts helping* MARK.

JOHN. And that special alcoholic's hangover. I pray you never get one. It's a fucking beaut. It's after a couple of days on the serious piss. What happens is, day one, for whatever reason, you've started early and basically polluted yourself. It's a form of poisoning. And so, on day two, you are in the absolute horrors. I don't mean what most people feel like after their Christmas party, sick tummy and a headache. This is a raging dose of the screaming paranoid shits. You're shit scared. Just to walk down the street you think you're going to be beaten up. And there's a sickening disgust with yourself to boot and there's only one thing you can do to stop it.

MARK. More drink.

JOHN. Bingo. On day two, you can get shitfaced very easily, because of all the alcohol your poor demented liver still hasn't had time to process, and neutralised. Technically you're still drunk. Oh but it's a bad drunk. So you'll feel okay after a few scoops, normal in fact, and ironically, not very drunk. You don't feel drunk. You feel normal. And you say to yourself, 'How brilliant it'd be to feel normal like this all the time and not need to get the booze into you at a horrifying rate.' But you know this feeling is going to go away, so you bale into a few more drinks. And then you begin to feel drunk. Drunk drunk. A bit euphoric and a bit fearless and generally a bit numb to all the bad feelings and the worries. But all the time there's the little niggle that it's going to disappear, so you won't even eat in case you might dilute the effect. And before you know it, you've passed out for two days in a row. Day three is a weird one. Well it always was for me. You've got the screaming paranoid shits back but your poor body is saying 'No more. I can't take it.' You'll puke if you tear into it. So you have to be a bit crafty and... sneak up on yourself. Lie on. Sleep it off a bit. Maybe eat a bit of a fry in the Kylemore or Bewley's or somewhere. And then, slowly, leisurely and generally a bit fucking nonchalantly have a few decent pints in a hotel bar or somewhere nice. Where you're not surrounded by a bunch of fucking mungos. And you'll be very tired but you won't be able to sleep. You'll just drowse enough to have a few terrifying dreams and wake up crying and all that. Day four you won't be so bad. But it won't long before day one rolls around again.

Short pause.

MARK. That sounds fucking awful!

JOHN. Yeah. Well. That's what Carol, the widow, that's what she was funding for me. She didn't know. She just wanted me to be happy. But massive highs and massive lows is not happy. Not in anybody's books. No. Noel has me sussed. I'm a mouth and a show off. He's calm. And not, just basically not a cunt about it. We'll go for a drink in the evenings. Granted, I'll drink twice as much as him. Say six pints to his two or three. But then it's into bed at a reasonable hour and you'll have had your tea and all that. So it's a stark contrast to the boys with the big sunburnt heads, having a belt off a bottle of meths before generally just sort of doing your toilet straight into your trousers.

JOHN *regards* MARK *for a moment.*

JOHN. Don't be worrying. Okay?

MARK. Yeah, I'm . . .

JOHN. I know. You just take it nice and handy now. I think you're probably a born worrier, are you?

MARK. I think I might be.

JOHN. Yeah. Do you know what would be brilliant? For you?

MARK. Yeah?

JOHN. Just to be incredibly fucking thick. Do you know what I mean?

They laugh.

JOHN. You know?

MARK. Yeah.

JOHN. Yeah . . .

MARK. You're not going to be on your own, are you? Tomorrow?

JOHN. I don't know. I suppose I was going to be. With Noel out of action. I was gonna go in and see him, you know?

MARK. We're going in in the morning. Me and Mum.

JOHN. Ah yeah. Good. Yeah I was gonna do that and then, I don't know. Watch the telly. But. I don't know. To tell you the truth, I'm not gonna get worked up about it. Tomorrow is Saturday and that's all. Another filthy morning, only there's a star in the East. Yeah. Is that it?

MARK. Nearly. The advent calendar.

JOHN. Oh yeah.

JOHN *goes and takes the advent calendar down from the wall.*

JOHN. They should have one of these with all year on it.

MARK. Yeah.

JOHN. With little words of wisdom. Little cautionary words of advice. The second of July. A word of caution. Fourth of August, a word to the wise. You know? November, 'You're being a spa, cop on to yourself, you know?'

MARK. A few jokes.

JOHN. A few jokes. Now you're talking. Mister Doom and Gloom over here. Are you going into town?

MARK. Yeah.

JOHN. You've enough money.

MARK. Yeah, I'm fine. Not gonna be too late anyway.

JOHN. Get into bed before Santa comes and checks.

MARK. And leaves me a bag of soot.

JOHN. Or slips Kim in your stocking.

MARK (*a slightly sad laugh*). Oh fuck.

JOHN. The imagination's gone fucko now.

> MARK *has his coat on. He takes out a Walkman and untangles the headphones.*

JOHN. Oh walkman! Noel gave me one a few Christmases ago. For sitting outside the church. You couldn't put the radio on in the hearse. It'd be awful, obviously. But you can slip in a little earphone, get the news and that. Yeah, great.

MARK. Yeah.

JOIIN. A woman singing in your car, ha?

> MARK *gives a little amused snort. He turns the tape in the machine over.*

JOHN. Do you have a radio on that?

MARK. Oh yeah. I think there's nearly radios on all of them now.

JOHN. You know if you're listening to the radio and there's all static and you put your hand on it.

MARK. Yeah, you earth it.

JOHN. Yeah and there's a clear signal. It'd be great to be able to do that, wouldn't it? To people, I mean. To people.

> *Short pause.*

MARK. Yeah.

JOHN. Go on. I'm losing the plot. Get outta here. Get out among the living.

MARK. I'll see you on Monday.

JOHN. Yeah there's some poor bastard out there. Looking forward to the old Xmas, not knowing he'll be under this roof on Monday waiting to be buried.

MARK (*a little laugh*). Could be you or me.

JOHN. Nah . . . (*Gives a little laugh.*) Go on, have a good time.

MARK. Okay.

They shake hands.

MARK. Happy Christmas. I'm sorry . . . for your wife.

JOHN. Yeah, Happy Christmas. Thanks. Don't eat too much cake.

MARK. Alright. I'll see you.

MARK *goes.*

JOHN (*calling after him*). And don't be worrying, do you hear me?

MARK (*off*). Yeah, I know.

JOHN *nods. We hear the outer door slam shut.*

JOHN *stands there for a moment and then looks around. He goes and takes a towel from a press and goes to the sink. He pauses and switches on a little transistor radio. Festive music is playing. He takes some soap and washes his face and neck and dries himself briskly.*

He fixes his tie carefully and puts on his jacket and overcoat. Then he takes a comb and does his hair in a little mirror. He is now ready. He stands there collecting himself.

He looks at the box of decorations. He considers them. He goes to the box and takes the advent calendar. He holds it for a moment and decisively places it back on the wall where it was. He returns to the box. He overturns it on the table. He selects some stuff and begins to put the decorations back up. He stands on a chair, redecorating. And from nearby the church bells chime out five o'clock.

The lights begin to fade. Then the music and the bells.

End of Part Three.

A Nick Hern Book

Dublin Carol first published in Great Britain in 2000
as a paperback original by Nick Hern Books Limited,
14 Larden Road, London W3 7ST, in association with
the Royal Court Theatre

Front cover photograph: Conor McPherson

Typeset by Country Setting, Kingsdown, Kent CT14 8ES

Printed in Great Britain by Bath Press, Avon

ISBN 1 85459 455 9